D1709127

FULL THROTTLE

LOWRIDERS

BY THOMAS K. ADAMSON

EPIC

BELLWETHER MEDIA · MINNEAPOLIS, MN

EPIC BOOKS are no ordinary books. They burst with intense action, high-speed heroics, and shadows of the unknown. Are you ready for an Epic adventure?

This edition first published in 2019 by Bellwether Media, Inc.

No part of this publication may be reproduced in whole or in part without written permission of the publisher. For information regarding permission, write to Bellwether Media, Inc., Attention: Permissions Department, 6012 Blue Circle Drive, Minnetonka, MN 55343.

Library of Congress Cataloging-in-Publication Data

Names: Adamson, Thomas K., 1970- author.
Title: Lowriders / by Thomas K. Adamson.
Description: Minneapolis, MN : Bellwether Media, Inc., 2019. | Series: Epic:
  Full throttle | Includes bibliographical references and index. | Audience: Ages 7 to 12.
Identifiers: LCCN 2018002178 (print) | LCCN 2018006497 (ebook) | ISBN
  9781626178731 (hardcover : alk. paper) | ISBN 9781681036205 (ebook)
Subjects: LCSH: Lowriders–Juvenile literature. | Automobiles–Customizing–Juvenile literature.
Classification: LCC TL255.2 (ebook) | LCC TL255.2 .A335 2019 (print) | DDC 629.222–dc23
LC record available at https://lccn.loc.gov/2018002178

Editor: Christina Leaf   Designer: Jeffrey Kollock

Printed in the United States of America, North Mankato, MN

TABLE OF CONTENTS

CAR
HOPPING

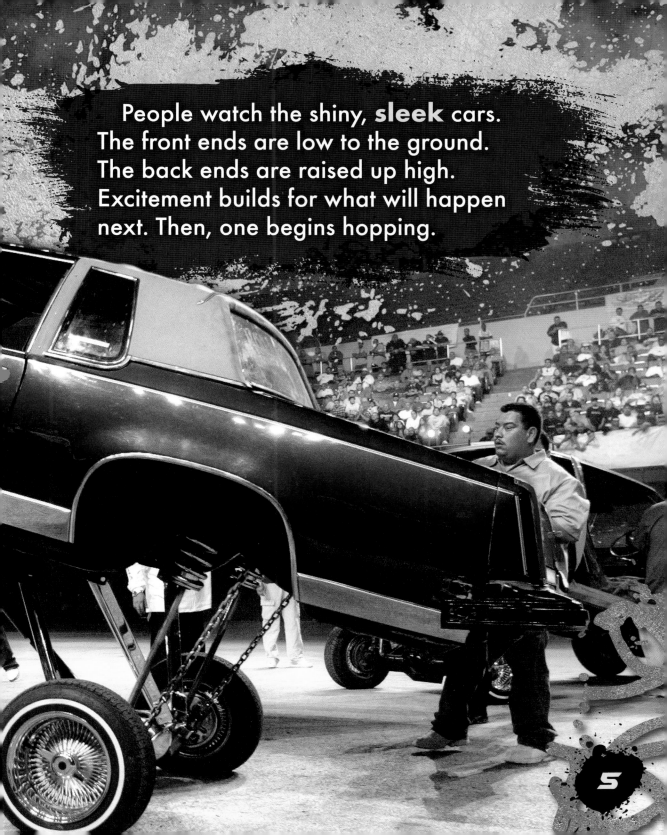

People watch the shiny, **sleek** cars. The front ends are low to the ground. The back ends are raised up high. Excitement builds for what will happen next. Then, one begins hopping.

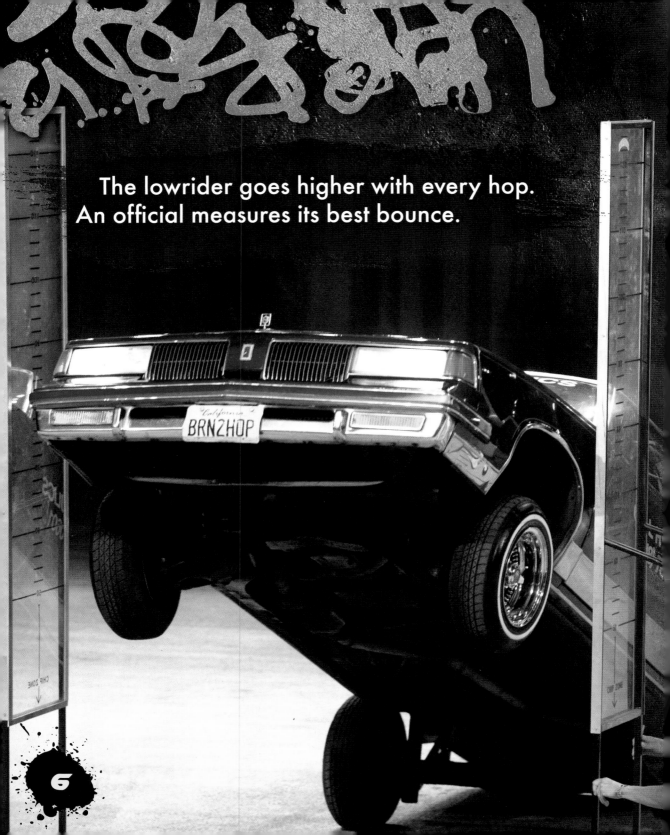

The lowrider goes higher with every hop.
An official measures its best bounce.

6

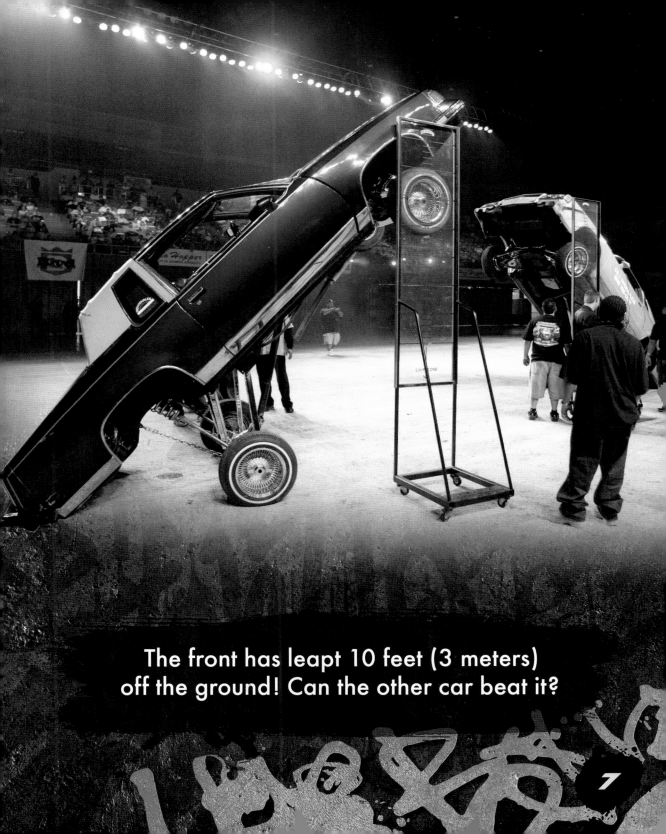

The front has leapt 10 feet (3 meters) off the ground! Can the other car beat it?

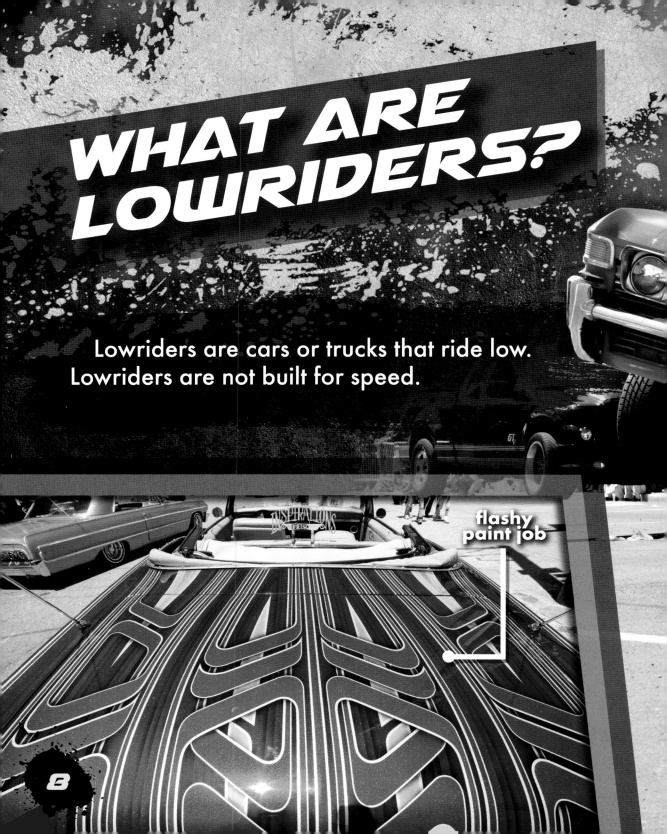

WHAT ARE LOWRIDERS?

Lowriders are cars or trucks that ride low. Lowriders are not built for speed.

flashy paint job

Owners try to make their lowrider
stand out. Flashy paint jobs show their **style**.

People with lowriders want their cool cars to be seen. They drive low and slow through city streets.

LOWRIDER BIKES
Lowriders are not always cars and trucks. People have made lowrider motorcycles and bikes!

For some, lowriding is a way of life.
Owners get together to talk about cars
and the community.

THE HISTORY OF LOWRIDERS

Lowriders started in the Mexican-American **culture** of the Southwest United States in the 1930s. Many people wanted classy-looking cars more than fast ones. Putting sandbags in the trunk made the back end ride low.

CLASSIC CHEVY

1939 Chevys gained popularity as lowriders after World War II. Their V-shaped fronts gave them a mean look.

1939 Chevrolet
Master Deluxe

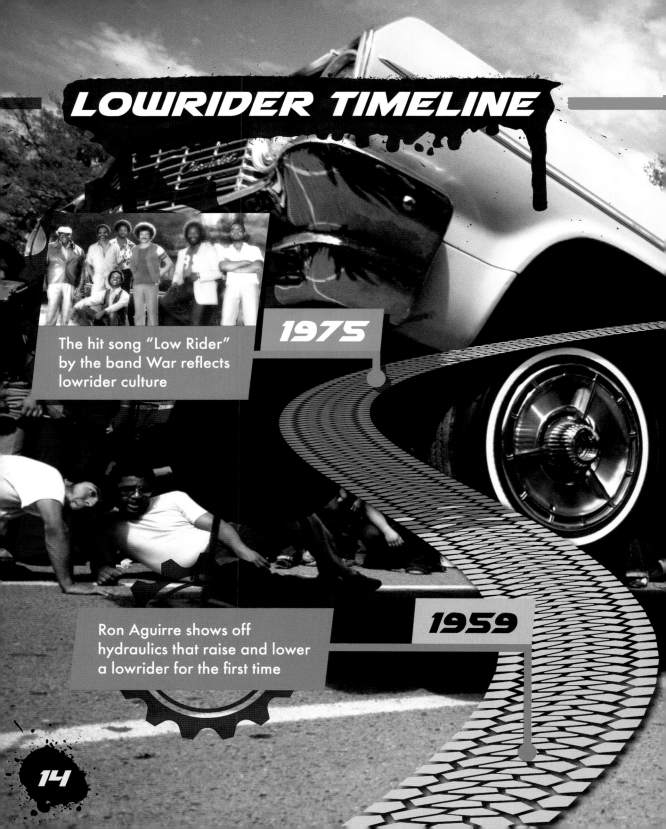

LOWRIDER TIMELINE

The hit song "Low Rider" by the band War reflects lowrider culture

1975

Ron Aguirre shows off hydraulics that raise and lower a lowrider for the first time

1959

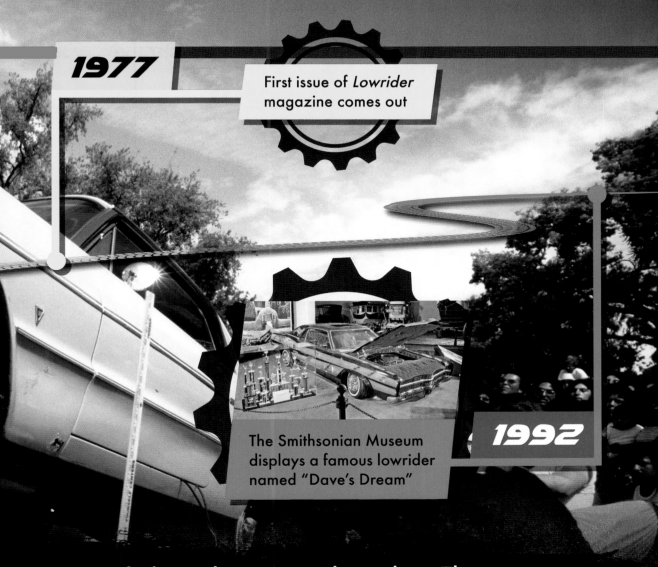

1977

First issue of *Lowrider* magazine comes out

The Smithsonian Museum displays a famous lowrider named "Dave's Dream"

1992

Early lowriders were Chevrolets. These cars cost little and were easy to repair. They looked more stylish than practical Fords. Today, 1964 Chevy Impalas are still common lowrider cars.

LOWRIDER PARTS

Lowriders rise up and ride low with special **suspensions**. They use air or **hydraulics** to raise and lower the car. Many lowriders have small tires. These tires make the car even lower. Fancy **rims** can add extra shine.

fancy rims

HOW LOW CAN YOU GO?

People used to make their car ride low by cutting springs in the suspension.

BLASTING THE SOUND

Lowriders are known for having great sound systems. Loud music makes people turn and look!

mural

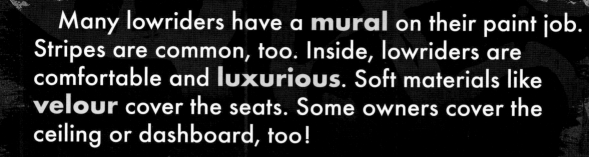

Many lowriders have a **mural** on their paint job. Stripes are common, too. Inside, lowriders are comfortable and **luxurious**. Soft materials like **velour** cover the seats. Some owners cover the ceiling or dashboard, too!

IDENTIFY A LOWRIDER

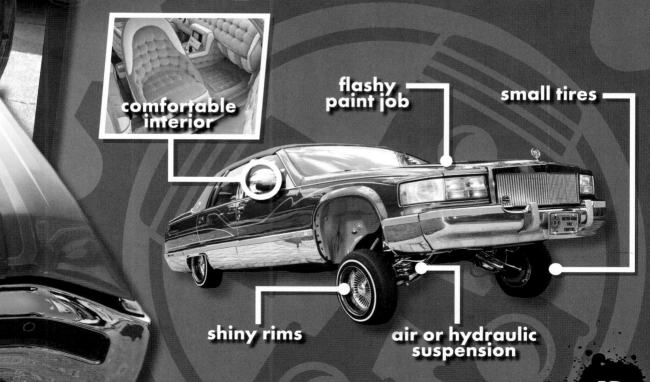

comfortable interior

flashy paint job

small tires

shiny rims

air or hydraulic suspension

LOWRIDER COMPETITIONS

LOWRIDER MOVES

Lowrider owners use a remote control to make their car do moves. Lowriders can dance from side to side, seesaw, or hop up and down.

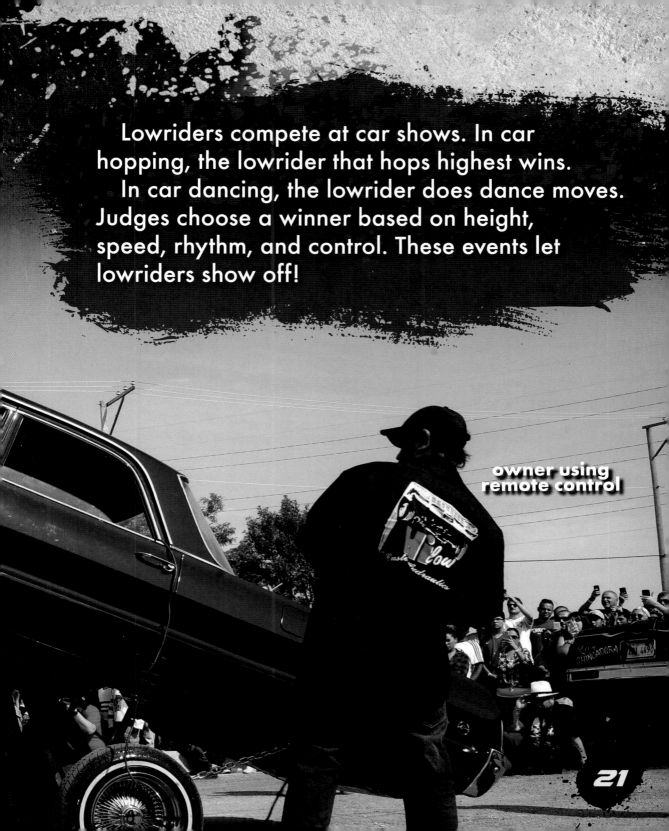

Lowriders compete at car shows. In car hopping, the lowrider that hops highest wins. In car dancing, the lowrider does dance moves. Judges choose a winner based on height, speed, rhythm, and control. These events let lowriders show off!

owner using remote control

GLOSSARY

culture—the ideas, traditions, and way of life of a group of people

hydraulics—machines that work on power that is created by liquid moving through pipes under pressure

luxurious—expensive and very comfortable

mural—a large painting done on the side of something, such as a wall or a car

rims—the outer round parts of wheels that the tire is mounted on

sleek—smooth and polished

style—a way of expressing oneself

suspensions—systems of springs, tires, and shocks that cushion a vehicle's ride

velour—a soft, velvety fabric

TO LEARN MORE

AT THE LIBRARY

Caswell, Deanna. *Lowriders*. Mankato, Minn.: Black Rabbit Books, 2018.

Mean Machines: Customized Cars. Tulsa, Okla.: Kane Miller, 2015.

Westcott, Jim. *Performance Cars*. Mankato, Minn.: Black Rabbit Books, 2018.

ON THE WEB

Learning more about lowriders is as easy as 1, 2, 3.

1. Go to www.factsurfer.com.

2. Enter "lowriders" into the search box.

3. Click the "Surf" button and you will see a list of related web sites.

With factsurfer.com, finding more information is just a click away.

INDEX

The images in this book are reproduced through the courtesy of: Flickr, front cover, pp. 1, 16; Ted Soqui/ Getty Images, pp. 4-5, 6, 7, 19 (interior); Judy Bellah/ Getty Images, p. 8; Suzanne Tucker, pp. 8-9; Roberto Galan, p. 10; Dave Parker/ Flickr, p. 11; Humberto Mendoza/ Lowrider Magazine, pp. 12-13; Stephanie Maze/ Getty Images, pp. 14-15; Wardrums/ Wikimedia Commons, p. 14 (War); National Museum of American History/ Smithsonian Institution, p. 15 (Dave's Dream); Michael Wheatly/ Alamy, pp. 16-17; Xinhua/ Alamy, pp. 18-19; CCE Hydraulics/ Flickr, p. 19 (lowrider); Victor Hilitski/ Newscom, pp. 20-21.